La Vecindad

A dream come true

Vanessa Barreat

La Vecindad

A dream come true

First edition, January 2022

La Vecindad, A dream come true

Copyright © 2022

Vanessa Barreat

Published by:

+1 702 559 5156

Las Vegas, Nevada.

United States Of America.

Dedication

*To that angel that guides me in life, but never taught me
how to live without her... my Mother!*

&

*To Chico and Bebé, my children... they are the most
beautiful story that destiny wrote in my life!*

Acknowledgments

Gratitude is the memory of the heart.

First of all, to God, to the universe, to energy! To all the good and the bad. To all the blessings and learning, to the energy that makes me vibrate high!

To Raul, my partner and husband, for his unconditional love, loyalty and for his passion in what he does!

To my children, for being my greatest motivation. For understanding our absence and valuing our presence!

To Erick Barreat, my brother, for believing in me!

To Erick Alejandro Barreat, my nephew, for making me feel important!

To Caesar's Palace, for being my school.

To Andrés Mendoza, "El Mitotero", from the first day always present with your love and support!

To Leaders Network Boost with Facebook for choosing us and opening the door to our only tool to make my business known in social networks.

*To Patricia Hernández Carrillo. " **You don't have to be better than others, but you do have to give your best.** "... Thanks to our coach for guiding us to perfect our talent. Teaching us that delivering*

Our Dharma to society makes us completely happy, because we are giving all our love and passion. When one works from what one loves, one is not working at all, one is only fulfilling one's Life Mission. Therefore, it is logical that if we give love through our service to others, we receive only good things in return.

To Paloma Makary, you arrived when we just opened. Without knowing who you were, you stopped being a customer and became a good friend!

To our great team: Luis Islas, Bartolomé Ortiz, Margarita Ortega, Oswaldo Tercero, Miguel Hernández, Yaiselis Medina, Gerardo Domínguez, Elíseo Macin, Frank Mejia, Don Jose Romero and Mardoqueo Santay for believing in us and being an important part of our Vecindad!

To Francisca Mojica, for your love and prayers!

To Denise Merida, for being and always being!

To our wonderful customers, we could not have grown without your support. Thank you for choosing us. The whole Neighborhood wants to convey to you that we work to continue to meet your expectations and, if possible, even exceed them. Your support and loyalty are what have allowed us to come so far, and what is to come!

Thanks to all those who supported us unconditionally. From being clients, to being very good friends and even being part of our family: LA VECINDAD.

"Blessed are those enlightened ones who come to us like an angel, like a hummingbird in a flower, who give wings to our dreams and who, having the freedom to leave, choose to stay and make a nest."

I love you all!

Vanessa Barreat

Prologue

When we see the realization of a dream, we hardly realize all that this achievement entails. Behind every dream achieved there is a sea of sweat, tears and effort, without which nothing would be possible.

The first time I visited La Vecindad Pico de Gallo I loved the atmosphere. It felt familiar. It smelled of freshly ground coffee, of laughter, of childhood memories. That impression became even stronger when I received my food.

Everything was perfect. The service, the ambiance and the products. To achieve this, Vanessa and her husband Raul have worked hard for many years.

This book reveals some of their strongest moments, where they were almost forced to give up on their dream, but thanks to their persistence, hard work and faith, they were able to overcome all obstacles, becoming recognized by important entities such as Facebook.

The learning we can take from Vanessa's experience is invaluable. Every aspect of her story teaches a little to those of us who, like her, want to achieve the elusive American dream.

This book is inspiration for those dreamers who want to make a difference. For those who are willing to pay the price to get what they long for.

I am sure this story will move many people to fight for their dreams and give their families hope for a better future.

Chapter 1

Believing with the mind and heart

What happens when we don't believe in ourselves? Who loses when I stop believing in myself? Without a doubt, I am the most affected, so take the plunge! believe in yourself, take the plunge, don't be afraid and don't doubt. Whatever it is, nothing is easy, if it were easy everyone would be an entrepreneur, everyone would have money, but this is what is going to make you different: What you believe. What will make you different from the rest, is yourself.

This is the story of how we started our dream, of how we believed to see our business become a reality. It has not been easy, but here we are.

We are in a free will, you are not poor because you were born poor, you are poor because you have not made the decision to change your life.

I learned, and I can say it now, that the decision is up to you. You can make the change, the tools are there, you have to prepare yourself and that starts from here inside. From the mind and the heart.

When you have that feeling that something is going to happen, that something good is going to come into your life, let it come to you. Believe. Trust. You have that conviction in your heart, you know something is going to come, but you don't know what it is. Just do it, believe it, because it magically happens.

We were given the opportunity to start our business in the Swapmeet. There were investments to be made and we had nothing. If it were for the money we had, we would never have started it.

Magically we thought we were going to get the money to start our business. We could have made the argument that we were not going to have anything to pay, but I firmly believed that I was going to have the money to make the monthly payments on a loan, because it was the only way to start that business, to build something. It was something for my family, something for me, for my children.

We took that loan despite the risk involved. We put everything on the line for the dream of having our business.

I no longer wanted to see my husband working every night, already tired, seeing that life was passing us by and we had done nothing.

No! There are things to fight for, there are things to improve, we just must work hard.

I remember that people came from abroad, from different countries and I never thought, I never imagined that, in such a small place, there in the market, there would be so many people. And yes! There were a lot of people. Don't ask me how, but it was that conviction that I had in my heart. I knew that my business had to be the best, to innovate, to do something different. What you think that maybe they are not going to accept, do it, because you are believing it. When we believe, extraordinary things happen.

We were the first ones to bring credit card devices, and within a week everyone was making credit card transactions at the food fair. That happened almost four years ago and now it is totally different, but because that is what it is all about, that you take a step and when you take the first step, the possibilities open for everything else to happen.

I can't tell you, no, it was scary, but it was worth it. When you are afraid to do something, do it, even with fear. Don't wait for it to pass because you never will if you wait around.

That was the beginning of what drove us to get to where we have gotten to this point.

I will tell you in the following chapters how we are doing, how it all happened. Now I can tell you that everything was totally divine, without a doubt it was God.

Chapter 2

Working Hard

I have seen that there are reasons for all this to happen, for it to materialize, for my children to feel proud of us, of what we are. They are aware that life is not easy. They go with us to work, they helped us clean. In fact, the big one helped us at the cash register when it was my turn to work. He would go with his dad to help him at the cash register, because sometimes Raul was alone, just with the lady making tortillas.

There are many things that happen when you are managing a business. Sometimes there are things that you can't control. For example, when one of the boys failed us, got sick and there was no other option but to tell him to stay home, even though you also felt sick, and you had to tell him: go home or don't come, and put on your pants and do it by yourself. At that moment you get strength from within, those internal forces that tell you that you have to get the job done and that it has to be done well, with or without strength, but it has to be done well.

"Pico de Gallo has a history, and in the beginning, it was hard work. Raul and I had two jobs, that is, we had the Swapmeet and while Raul was still working at night, I was also still working my eight hours at the casino.

I woke up the same as I do now, at five in the morning, with the illusion that we were doing something that we did not know what it was, but we did have that inner feeling, that little inner confidence that something good was going to happen next, that the miracle was going to happen. What? We had no idea, but it was going to happen.

Chapter 3

An Opportunity

They say that there is a rule that a business begins to bear fruit after two years; but in the first year almost everyone throws in the towel. No money came out of the Swapmeet to pay that loan, I paid that loan with my other job, because we did not have the money or the capacity to say: we are going to do it! But it is a challenge.

A lot of people made fun of us, they said: "These assholes are not going to make it" and they told us so, that was what challenged me. That's what challenged me, I must keep going! We must move forward! and "these assholes" are going to make a difference, I don't know how, I couldn't even imagine how, but I knew, we had to do it. Today I can say that thanks to the job I had, I was encouraged to do something, I was encouraged to create a business together with my husband.

When I was in the Swapmeet I saw the first year, then the second year, and I was already uncomfortable with the fact that I had to check the blessed weather to know if we could do business every day, because in the Swapmeet we could only make sales when the weather was good. I could only see Raul's face and I could tell it was going to rain. If there were thirty or forty miles of wind, that would damage our weekend or workday. Sometimes on Sundays, which were the best days for us, we didn't do anything because people didn't go because it was too windy. I mean, who is going to be walking around in that weather!

That's when I told Raul: look daddy, now! We have to do something else.

He said to me, "What do you want China? He thought I wanted to close, but I didn't. That was the only way to pressure him, to make him see that we had to decide and take the next step. That was the only way to pressure him, to make him see that he had to decide and take the next step.

I told him: Daddy, I'm tired, I'm tired, I'm fed up with this.

At that time, we were not making money, but it wasn't really about that. I wasn't going to give up, I wasn't going to keep the idea that I could have done something more, it was in my mind that I had to keep fighting. For me giving up was not an option. It was about doing what was necessary to keep growing.

So, I said to him: We must look for a place, I want to have my own business, let's look for a location. He said to me: "China, you are crazy! And so it seemed, because we still had no money, we were still without that money in the bank to say we are going to rent a place.

To look for a space in a shopping center we had to have good credit and several thousand dollars for payments and deposit, and we didn't have that. Many things like that were said to us, and it seemed that it was impossible for us.

So, we kept on thinking about the idea of being in a store. On one occasion I told Raul: "You know what? Leave the business to Chapo (as a thank you, because he was the only one who believed in us and kept working with us until the last moment) and we had promised Chapo that if we did well, he would do well too, and we told him: You know what Chapo? The day we are going to leave this place, we are going to leave it to you, and obviously we were going to keep our word. But we were also going to leave a business to a person who was the same or worse off than us, that is, without a penny. Where was the poor guy going to get it if he didn't have any? We were going to receive money from Chapo, but we had to give him time and since we also went through there, we were blessed to be able to generate money, but it was going to cost him a little more.

So, we continued the same way, working, opening. A customer from Swapmeet called us to tell us: why do we have to wait until the weekend to have to eat with you? Look for your location, you are ready, you are an eminence, you already have a lot of experience, jump in the water!

This is what they told us, and we were thinking inside: yes, jump into the water, but nobody can imagine all that is involved in jumping into the water! But we did get that little worm of restlessness in us, and we said: why not?

Raul took the plunge. I had the confidence inside me that something was going to happen, something was going to come. I didn't know what, I thought that maybe we could rent inside someone else's restaurant or something like that. So many things went through our heads! But we never thought of doing a partnership, that never crossed our minds, but we had nothing.

One day a client who called us on the weekends to buy some chickens called us. He called Raul to tell him that he had someone who was delivering a store, so Raul told me: China, let's go see him! I was apathetic, because I knew what the process was like, and I knew they were going to start asking for things, so I thought it was a waste of time. But we went anyway.

When we went to see the place, there was no light. They showed it to us without lights, and we said: "It's spectacular! They sold it to us as a gold mine, but it was a transfer and that transfer was going to cost us 20 thousand dollars, for moving to a place that was supposedly ready to open. They told us that due to an emergency the person needed to transfer it quickly and wanted the money fast.

Imagine that! We, ignorant, ignorant in the sense of not knowing anything about what it meant to open our own location, did not check what is important when you go to see a place and we fell in love with the place. We arrived, opened that door, and said: Here it is! It's ready, we just turn on the light and open it.

Without asking, we went to the office, we made the transfer, I gave the money to the boy, we went to the manager's office, in other words, everything was so easy, totally different from what we had already been told about what it meant to rent a location in a shopping mall. We thought we already had our own business, ignoring everything that was behind it. I signed papers; we took out the legal documents where I was committing myself to answer for the rent of this place. In many places the rent was very expensive, around four or five thousand dollars, and obviously we had to look for a place that we had to pay for no matter what. That is why we took advantage of that opportunity, because the rent was practically half of what they normally charged, and we said: This is it! Whether there is business or not, even if it is selling on the street, but I must make up the rent and we could do it, so I signed.

They gave us the keys, we went in, I connected the electricity. Supposedly they were giving me all the permits to start up.

I started to make the corresponding calls to get everything going, that we had to go to get the permit, we had to pay. When we went

what about this man? I dialed him again, I said: what is the problem? He answered me angrily: "That place will not open without my signature, I mean, you are not going to open!

But what are you talking about? -I said, not understanding. The man gave me an insult, he told me: for you to be able to open, you will have to get a contractor and you will have to make a grease trap, but this way, you won't open.

The guy hung up on me again and I didn't know what he was talking about. I start to investigate, to see what was going on, and it turns out that they had transferred a business to me that had had problems with permits, that they could not start it because they did not have enough resources to do it, it was easier for them to transfer it, to keep their mouths shut, to grab the first suckers that passed by and deceive them and wash their hands and that is what they did with us.

Imagine that! Without money, because obviously to rent this place, to pay for this transfer, I went to the bank again and asked for another loan to pay this guy because I wanted his money now.

So, I had already paid the first loan, for that reason I went to ask for the second one for the rent, first it was the lease, so imagine having paid money that went to the trash. So what do I do? -And I thought: "Well, you're not going to see my stupid face, this business is opening.

It had been a month waiting for an answer, nobody had told us anything. Raul starts painting, we start decorating our place, but we thought it was not going to take long, but we never imagined how much time it was going to take.

And then the Water Reclamation thing happens, and he tells me a contractor, which is an architect, or a person that you pay to take care of all the permits, whatever it is, it's like you call a licensed construction and he takes care of finalizing all the details so that the business or whatever it is that you are going to open is in optimal conditions.

That implied an expense of more than 60 thousand dollars, and where were we going to get that money from? I went to the family of the boy who transferred the business to us, I told him what happened, and he told me: do not worry, everything is ready, call this person, it is already advanced, he is going to help you, it is already arranged, you do not have to pay anything.

When I called the "architect" I had to pay him, it was almost 3,500 dollars that I had to pay that man to make some plans and deal with the Water Reclamation inspector who had thrown the phone at me.

Yes, he helped us. Thanks to that, from 60 thousand to 3,500 and without having any money, but at least that information helped me to solve what was happening, what they could not do because they cheated me, because for me it was a deceit what they did, and I talked to this architect, I explained the situation, he told me: Don't worry, I'm going to help you, I know that inspector, I'm going to look for the turns so you don't have to do the grease traps, give me time, and this give me time is to call him every day because they are people who are super busy, you are depending on them but they don't depend on you, they have a lot more people to be working and they go by order, that is, if they have time they solve your issue.

And weeks and weeks would go by, and I would call him again: what happened? have you managed to talk to him yet? He would answer no, I am still making the plan, he has not given me an appointment, I am waiting, I am here in the city, in other words, a never-ending story, until I finally told him: you know what, we have been waiting for three months and nothing.

I remember that the manager of the mall called me and said: Vanessa, don't keep working, stop, because I don't think you are going to open. -I told her: but we are painting. -She said to me: Can I ask you a question, did you pay the person who gave you the place? -And I said: yes. -She just shook her head, because she had realized that we had been robbed and she said to me: don't stop, wait at least to get an answer from the architect at Water Reclamation to know if this is going to start.

I told her: Cheryl, we put in what we didn't have for this, we can't stop, it can't end here! - And he said: Vanessa, if you want, I can help them with half of what it would cost you to make a grease trap, we are talking about 30 thousand.

The architect was able to get the inspector's signature approving the use of the Big Dipper. If we replaced it with a new unit. Which cost us $6000. Then the next step was the Fire Department permit. When the Fire Marshall came there was an electrical problem, this was a Friday. The Marshall very kindly gave me his cell phone number, giving me a chance to fix the problem that same day, but it took longer. We were against the clock, because the Health Department was coming on Monday after this inspection, and we needed the signed sheet from the Marshall approving the location!

He said: don't worry, I am going to send an email to my partner, so that before the Health Department arrives on Monday morning, he will check on you so that you have the whole weekend to fix it.

Genaro, who is the person who helps us with all these little things, woke up working. At about one or two in the morning he sent us a message, letting us know that he had been able to fix it. Saturday morning, I called the Marshall, a man who doesn't even know me, I guess he saw my desperation and didn't answer. On Monday at 7 a.m. he sent me a message: Vanessa, that paper that I left you on Friday already has my signature, since Friday you were already approved. I just wanted to make sure that you fixed it.

The Health Department arrived at 10 o'clock in the morning. When they came in, they just said, "Wow, you guys did a great job here.

It looks like they had come before and saw what the place was and what we had transformed it into, from the front door to the last corner of the kitchen, and all they said was: Congratulations, you are ready to open!

And we set the opening date with excitement. It was crazy to open, even though we had been working at Swapmeet for two years, but imagine opening something formal, something that people go to with the expectation of seeing what you are going to do or what mistakes you are going to make. We invited people, mostly friends that we thought were going to be there with us and our biggest surprise was that the people we least expected to be there were the ones that were present at our opening. Those who we thought would be there never showed up and to this day have not arrived.

Raul has many friends who have tried to do business, who even did business, and threw in the towel because they didn't make it. We had options to go to eat anywhere, we went to them just to support them, to help them, to say here I am, I am going to support your business. We thought: maybe those people are going to be there with us too. Raul was very disappointed. They were never there and to this day they have not come.

But it's a learning experience. The blow is hard. To realize that there are people who believe in you, others who make fun of you, and people who say: another asshole! If I didn't do it, you're not going to do it. Because that's what they said. Of those who laughed, of those who told Raul when you can, when you open you give me a job as a manager, you give me a job. My biggest surprise was that it was all mockery.

The day we opened we looked like spinning tops; we didn't know what was going on, running, bumping into each other, taking orders. We had a cash register that was there, it had been there for years and that was the one we used because where were we going to find the money to buy one ourselves, it was a dinosaur. We rehearsed how to enter the prices and how to charge.

Raúl was cooking and he came to help us take out plates, well, we looked like crazy, trying to get the job done.

If there were people on the first day, which surprised me, those same people who supported us were going to eat with us at the Swapmeet. Many had not returned to the Swapmeet, even though they liked our food, because they were too lazy to go in. That's when another learning curve began, how to organize ourselves.

I called people who had worked with me when I was a manager at a fast-food restaurant and they came with me and worked with us. They helped us to clean, to close. People who were part of the learning process, who were there at that time.

Everything is presented at the level that you grow, there are several stages through which "Pico de Gallo" went through.

In this first stage these people were crucial, because they were part of our beginnings and I thank them for working for me, I thank them for having supported us to start, with people who put a lot of heart, they worried about everything going well, so that everything would be ready in case they came to inspect us.

It was not easy to open the business, to come to open the business, to arrive in the morning, one or two clients arrived. You have the illusion that you have opened your business, but imagine opening it for people to arrive and almost no one arrives...

Chapter 4

Shaping the dream

There are people who turn their backs on you. Sometimes it is the same family members with whom things happen. We thought we were going to be fine, because with Raul, we love each other, we love each other, we have children and we are still together, we wanted to do business for their future and because we wanted to do something together.

There was something that did not let us, as if we had to cure it, but we did not know what. That was separating us, it was causing us internal problems and I didn't care anymore, I didn't even know if we should go on with the business, but we went on anyway.

At that time, we were about to celebrate our one year anniversary, but we were holding on, holding on, because they say that after two years is when a business supposedly starts to bear fruit. We were just holding on to that hope.

They asked us if we were going to celebrate the first anniversary, and the truth is we didn't have anything to celebrate with. What are we going to celebrate without money? And things started to happen in my family, my mother got sick, in other words, family things: mine and his.

Beautiful people started to arrive, telling us: "Go for it, the food is very tasty!

Those comments, although small, inspired us to keep going. I thought well, we seem to be doing well here. People started a little bit at a time, but they were going. It was when we started to make a little more money of 300, 400, 500, 600 dollars, it went up a little bit and that is when I remember that a guy arrived and brought a girl who offered me her services as a coach.

I didn't believe in such things. Coach of what? -I thought. But I talked to him. We were introduced, but at that moment I didn't understand what it was, what it was for, but I was interested.

I said yes, but I didn't say yes for me, but for Raúl, for everything we were going through and because he needed that something more to believe it; I needed him to be stronger, because I felt a very heavy weight on me, I felt that all the weight was on me.

That's when Patricia Hernandez Carrillo, the mentor, the Coach, offered me a package that included a couple of sessions, a video and I don't know what else. And I said: well, this is how I got Raul to start working, because I knew it was necessary, that if we didn't do this, the business would collapse, and my family would collapse. When I say my family, I am talking about my marriage and my children, because there were already many factors influencing our lives and that, in one way or another, was what prevented our business from starting.

With stress, you have a limit, you think you have reached a limit and you think you are not going to go up, and besides all the obstacles involved in having a business, it is not easy. Suddenly you want to throw in the towel, but at the same time you say: I have already gone through all this, am I going to throw in the towel? am I going to give up? And that's when I took courage and said: we need help.

We knew there was something else to do, and that something else was to prepare ourselves mentally, emotionally and physically for what was coming, because it is not easy to have a business, that is why I learned that many businesses do not go ahead, because of the emotional part, but that is the magic part that makes the difference and by faith they move away from people who get stressed, who get sick, who say: this is not for me, I am not going to continue, I better stay with my eight-hour job, my paycheck, my vacation once a year and with that I am happy.

Little by little we regained confidence, again to tell our mind: I do not want to throw in the towel, I am not going to go back with the boards in my head and give people the pleasure of saying they did not do it.

And we kept going, we kept going with lows and highs, but we kept going and that's when we started working with our mentor. It's been a good process, and when you develop to move up a level it's one step at a time. Doing whatever it takes, because opportunities present themselves and as you move up, doors open, your mind opens, and you get the light, you get the creativity, you get the desire, I would wake up in the morning and say: this is what we are going to do, this is what I must do! But it is because you need that key, you need that push that says, keep going, keep going, keep going, you can do it.

When we started working with our mentor we realized many things, you find the why and the what for, and when she gives you all these tools to open another path for you, and to make things happen, you begin to understand that everything is part of that energy of love that you feel for yourself, and for what surrounds you, that you are no longer you if it is not everything, it is a whole, it is that you are no longer in a position that you just have to prepare yourself, not to help yourself, but to go to a higher level because you have to help others.

For that you have to prepare yourself emotionally, grow and realize what you are, what you are worth, to know that you have to believe it is not easy, to know what you are, what you have to do and understand that your business is you, it is what you have created, it is that energy that will make you move forward, that energy that starts to reach people on your own. That what you are feeling is what people receive and when you understand and when you know that there is a lot of good vibes involved and that this good vibes and this good energy that you are transmitting makes more people keep coming and that the walls of your business talk, that the walls of your business feel, when you understand that your business is also energy, that is not easy to explain, but when you prepare yourself, you generate it. That's where the secret is: what you transmit. Because you already managed to overcome one obstacle, and you overcome the first one, but it turns out that the next one is waiting for you.

You think that one is the easiest and it happens that the universe tells you that you are a supergirl, but it is not to make you stronger, because it is not how you do it, but if you achieve it. The important thing is to get there and be thankful, I think the magic word is thank you.

Thanks to all those angels who taught you and who appear in your life to give you strength to move forward. It is not easy, but the hardest thing we did was to open it and you think: everything will be easy, but no, now comes the hardest part: to start building your business.

I loved my job, but I knew there was something more, I didn't want to stay there. I saw jobs at Caesars Palace and there are many people there who have been working their whole lives for thirty or forty years, those ladies come with their walkers to work. Most of them were older people. I thought about what their lives meant: coming in every day, waiting, working so hard for a pension, for insurance, and I didn't want to be one more, I didn't understand why those people were there.

To have worked all your life and still must keep working because you have to secure your paycheck for when you're old or to have health insurance, it's not my thing.

I knew I had to do something else, I knew it was time to change jobs, I knew I had reached my limit, and there came a time when I would come home from work and say: This is not what I want.

I didn't want to continue working for the rest of my life to be an ordinary person, I am different, I did it because I am different, I did it because I know I have the capabilities to do it, because if others have business, why not me? I don't have money, but I can have it because I learned that it's not where you are, it's who you are.

I always knew that you are like who you surround yourself with, who you rub shoulders with. If you surround yourself with enterprising people, if you surround yourself with people who want to get ahead, who want to create, who want to have money, who are millionaires, I think that's what you're going to do.

If you surround yourself with poor people, with mediocre people, with negative energy, you are going to absorb that.

One of the reasons I've pretty much always been alone is because I've been very independent. I can't be with a person who suddenly doesn't believe in who I am. I always felt that I had to do something else, I had to do something else, I had to make a difference.

When I started to open my business, I used to laugh because people would ask me, "How do you do it? I don't know, I do it. It's something I was born to do. To work eight hours standing up, imagine it is a feeling, then to leave work, to come here, how do you do it, you must arrive dead. And I answer: no, look, I was dead when I was working eight hours without hope of a different future.

When I arrived at my business, I changed my mentality and it was as if I was filled with energy, as if I had just woken up. For me to be working eight hours was to be asleep, it was not me and that is why I did it. That is why I supported Raul, that is why I told him that I believed in him, and I was going to support him, because I also loved him, I also believed in him, I knew there was going to be something else, I did not know what it was, but I knew it was something else.

Something told me that I was going to do something special. When famous artists began to arrive, I saw that contact with people. That of being known, renowned, that fulfilled me, it was my thing, but I'm not a model and I'm not an artist either, but I saw myself in that environment of recognition. How was I going to achieve it? I didn't know how I was going to reach people and the fact of starting my business was what started to change my reason. It was for my children, to make them proud of themselves and their family.

My kids are very smart, I was blessed with kids that I don't have to be on top of them to do homework. They were tested for being child prodigies, they call them in Spanish; they are children that have an incredible cognitive ability, and I could not stay behind, I had to show them that they had to be proud of their parents, that they can do anything, if we do it they will do it too.

I have taught them that they must be independent, I have taught them that they should not count on anyone or expect anything from anyone to get ahead and they know it. They value and are aware of the work their parents are doing, because it is not just any job, it is not just anything we are doing, and that fills them with pride.

The fact that seeing mommy on TV or in the newspaper or daddy's picture also together in the newspaper here in Vegas, that fills them with pride, their eyes shine or when they see me doing my videos on Facebook or tik tok, they laugh: "you are crazy" - they say. But it's to show them that it's not impossible, they have it on a silver platter, but they know their parents are not Americans, they are immigrants who had many obstacles, like the language.

They correct me when I say something wrong in English. They tell me: Mommy, that's not how you say it, you say it this way. And I tell them: No, I say it the way I want, I am not an American citizen, but you are. -But it's so that they know that despite our limitations, that didn't stop us from doing what we are doing.

They have seen us cry, they have seen us angry, they have seen us frustrated, frustrated in the sense that we don't know if we are going to make it. Sometimes they ask: How was your day today? And I answer them: more or less, it wasn't so busy my love, but it doesn't matter, let's eat.

They have been part of this process and now that they are surprised, it feels so nice, it feels a satisfaction that, in these days, when they knew, we were going to expand, as they are in the house with all the COVID, locked up, they had not seen with their own eyes all that we have achieved in this time. When they came, they understood why we were not at home.

Raul tells me: because here where we are right now at the bar, we are expanding in pandemic time, the craziest thing you could ever hear, such a small business expanding in pandemic time when businesses are closing.

My kids came here to help, to pick up to prepare for an event we were going to have and when they saw this, they didn't believe it.

They didn't say anything, but there was something in their eyes. The surprise they felt at that moment and the most beautiful thing was that that weekend there was a line, there were people outside waiting to come in and Raul says he felt so good that my son, the little one, peeked through the door and said: "Boy, boy, come see. There are people waiting to come in. They were proud to see that the business, people were waiting to come in, Facebook also sent us an invitation to be on a television program on Univision News, they were going to do a report on how such a small business in times of pandemic was expanding and people were coming to eat. I participated in that interview and when they saw it, they screamed in the house, "Mommy is on TV,

Mommy is on TV! And they said: Mommy, you are famous. I said: no, son, not yet, and they just hugged me, and it was something special, but that hug was a hug of pride and that is the most comforting thing, to know that they realize that all the work we have done has been worth it, that we are receiving or reaping what we have worked so hard for, and that we deserve this.

That fills them up and they look forward to us. We arrive almost at midnight, and they are just waiting for us to give us a hug and go to sleep. It is gratifying that we got home and that it was a fruitful day and that is priceless.

You teach them that, that they have to do their best, that their parents are not ordinary, that whatever they do they have to do their best, and that is what I get from them, I am completely sure that they are on their own doing their best and the result is in their grades at school, and it is also their turn to help us.

It's their turn to help me clean up, they must wash their dishes, to wash their clothes, to fold them and they help us in the house, but it's also their turn to work because they are not going to sit all day until we arrive. They know that we are not sitting here, we are working, and they are doing the same at home; they finish their classes and start doing their activities. Afterwards they must help to arrange their rooms, and lately I don't have to tell them anything, I just get home and they start to tell me: Mommy, did you notice that I did this or that? And it feels nice, because they know that mom and dad are here working hard and are aware of what we are doing.

That's why we have done all this because we don't want to be the same as everyone else, waiting for a check, you feel that in here, if you know there is going to be something else, you don't know what it is, but you do it, and that's what has led me to move forward. I don't think we're all the same, but at least we do our best to get by.

But all I can say is that my children are my biggest motivation, sometimes I wonder if they know what we are doing, and I realize that they do. It also feels nice that people realize that we have worked hard, that it is not to say that we have a business, it is something more, it is something more than saying that you have a business. It is what you feel and to create something different and that is how everyone should be, that is, that there is a feeling, that there is support, which is what humanity needs. We need humanity, we need love, we need sincerity, we need to want to help you and to want to share, and I share this to inspire you?

Once someone commented to my husband that my posts or the things, I uploaded from my business on Facebook looked very professional. I took it as a compliment, but then they criticized because I even put the logo, and said why did I do that? Why did he put the logo, that people like the ordinary, that, because he did it that way, and that had worked for him? But weeks later he was putting the logo on his posts, which was what Raul criticized me for doing.

A week later he was doing it, then you say: you criticize me, and it turns out that a few days later you are doing what I am doing, so what are you playing at? How hard it is for you to say: I like your work; you are doing it well. I liked your idea. I would like to do it too, but no. He criticized it and then he was doing the same thing. Well, he tried to do it better.

I continued to work on my networking by putting on Facebook, using Instagram, I tried Snapchat, but I didn't like it. I went back again with Facebook and Instagram and I was always active, active, active.

One day my phone rang and they told me it was Facebook and I thought they wanted to fool me, they wanted to see my stupid face, I thought it was a scam, people who just wanted to trick me and told me: Hello, we are from Facebook, we want you to be part of a group of national leaders of small businesses

and we would like your business to be part of
our team.

It was too good to be true. Because I was
already so disappointed with everything that
had happened, he said, we're going to take
you in for an interview. I thought: let's see
what they are going to come up with, let's see

how much they want to charge me, that's what I thought, that it was another deception, because unfortunately disappointments do that to you, they make you more doubtful, they make you more astute, more cunning, more alert, that they are not going to see your face again and that's what I thought with this call.

The day I had made the appointment that person was very punctual; my phone rang, and I hesitated for a second to take the call because that's what I do when I see that they are scam or companies that want to bother or want to sell you something. I prefer not to answer, and I never go to the phone to avoid them also the bad time that I am going to answer and tell them no, but for God's sake I answered the phone.

I answered the call, and it was them. They told me: "We are going to ask you some questions. They asked me about the history of the business, among other key questions. I don't know what I said or what they saw in what I was doing that seemed so special that they told me: you will receive an email from

Facebook inviting you, you accept, you sign the contract, and I don't know what else. I was still waiting to see how much it was going to cost me because I thought that is not free.

They send me the welcome email, they make another phone call to tell me that it is official that "La Vecindad, Pico de Gallo" was part of the Facebook Leaders Network in the United States.

They told me the steps I had to take to be part of their network and to be aware of everything that was happening there. I still had not figured out what was going on. I start to see, I give "I like", we start to contact, they communicate me with one of the main moderators of that team and I start to see everything. It's like a school, but free. They give you information before it goes out on Facebook, they are already participating us as small businesses, how we must prepare ourselves, from how we have to do, what they recommend us, how we have to make the posts, that you have to use the tools, everything that you see later I already know, because Facebook sends it to me.

I didn't get what I had received, I didn't believe it, I took it as something normal, I didn't give it importance.

It turns out that, about a week later, I received a package in the mail. That package was like a welcome to Facebook as a small business and brought a welcome letter, a cap, and a lot of little details that I said, it's true this is from Facebook, this is directly, that's when I realized that it was really Facebook that was behind all this.

Months later they call me and tell me that there is going to be a nationwide advertising campaign; this advertising campaign is going to go from coast to coast. It is going to carry only 45 business names. Imagine, in the United States there are millions of small businesses, and it turns out that they were only going to choose 45 and among those 45 the name of my business was going to be there. I did not believe it, it was very special to me and that same week they sent me an invitation to Washington, where I was going to be in the name of my business, with this group of national leaders exchanging and learning. Sharing the story of my business in Washington on behalf of Facebook, for me that was amazing, to be the only small business, Mexican restaurant as small as mine, and that Facebook has taken us into account, for me that is a blessing, first because my English is not perfect, and there what is there is pure American.

There are only a few Hispanic people there and most of them are from the east coast, nothing to do with this side. Only from California and in Las Vegas nothing else, practically as Hispanic America is us, it is a pride. I felt important and what I have learned with them is what I show in the pages. I was very excited that I was going to travel, but the pandemic happened, and the trip had to be postponed. I could not travel to Washington in April because of the pandemic and the advertising campaign was also cancelled, also because of the pandemic, so my spirits dropped a little bit, I had mixed feelings, like saying they gave it to you and they took it away, but it is also part of the process. I kept going and I say it to the four winds, social networks are the only thing that can help you with small businesses, even big ones, use the networks, make programs, do not be afraid.

Invest in your business. If a TV channel tells you that it is $3,000 to $5,000 for an advertising campaign or a radio station $500 to $1,200, don't spend it. If you spend a tenth of that money on Facebook, you're going to do a lot better.

Play with the tools, make videos to people, believe it or not people love that.

When we had to close, we were like that for two months because of the pandemic. That's when social networks were fundamental.

We had to warn that we were going to be closed for a month. We closed with tears in our eyes because it was only in this first quarter of this year when we literally recognized that we were receiving our first fruits, that is, we could say that we were no longer using our credit card, now we were only paying what we owed all this time and that this happened was a low blow.

Facebook itself advised us to keep in touch, not to stop promoting. We kept in touch with people, we kept talking to clients, I would post one thing or another from time to time, I kept promoting posts.

Sometimes I would say: "I'll stop? But it wasn't much, it was $10. I was investing about two dollars a day, but I was closed and not producing any money. In the long run it was money that I didn't know if I was going to need. I doubted if I should also pay for Facebook promotions, but I kept going. The first week we were disappointed, Raul and I were locked up at home, but then we looked each other in the face, and we said to ourselves: why are we locked up with our arms crossed? Let's do something! And that's when we decided to go back to the business and started painting.

He started first in the sky, we began to make the fresh water cart, we made a little corner for our souvenirs and all that I was informing people on Facebook and Instagram, I was telling them what we were doing, we knew that this was going to be temporary, and we told them: look what we are doing for you, that even though we were closed, we kept the illusion that we could reopen.

Of course, with the same fear that we did not know if we were going to have to close for good. For a moment we thought that we had reached that point, for a moment we thought that everything was going to end, and we could no longer fight against the current, because they were no longer simple factors, but major factors.

We were in a pandemic that caused the whole economy to collapse, so these are things that make you think and I told Facebook what I was doing.

The governor announced on Thursday that we could open on Saturday. He said: this Saturday the restaurants can open, only 50%, and I asked Raul: what do we do, do we open or leave it closed? And Raul said to me: China, we better open on Monday. We did not open immediately on Saturday, but I informed all our customers on the networks that we were preparing; we were going to clean, to make sure they received freshness and quality.

We let them know what was going to happen on Monday and we fearfully kept cleaning. We were getting ready. I met with the guys, we rethought how we were going to proceed, how we were going to do with the people, and we told the team: I don't know what is going to happen here, we don't know what is going to happen tomorrow, but, we are going to continue giving our best.

Our biggest surprise was that we turned on the warning light and the boom was unbelievable. We were busier than when we closed. It seems that there was no pandemic, it seems that they were preparing us for all this that was coming, illogical that in time of pandemic we are busy, that we broke our sales record that, from making 300 dollars, we sold everything in one day.

We were setting goals and after we reopened with the pandemic, we had the luxury of overcoming every challenge we set for ourselves. We reopened in June, and we said: this month we are going to sell so much, and we broke records; in July, August we are going to sell so much, and we surpassed the goal we had set and so on, and all this magically, all this thanks to the blessing of having so many beautiful people supporting us.

That's why they did that interview with me, so when we opened after we were ordered to close everything, instead of closing our doors, we had nowhere to seat people.

People had to wait in line to get in. They would spend hours out there; they would even leave angry because they couldn't get in to eat with us. Many people don't believe it, even we didn't believe it ourselves, but how to organize so many people, so much so that instead of cutting personnel I had to take on more staff to be able to manage and continue offering the same quality and the same service.

Even a musician, so that when people came in, they would not be stressed but relaxed, always thinking about that, about energy, about making them feel good.

We were much more active, making videos, one of the chefs I worked with is excellent, that is, he was my perfect team to be more active in the networks and to win over those people who were on their phones.

During the pandemic there were a lot of people who were on their phones, on the networks, they were watching what was happening in the world, they didn't want to watch TV and instead of watching TV they watched social networks. So, they had your advertising in their hands, easy and cheap.

Be always active is my advice, post two, three things a day, answer your messages, answer people, and show yourself as you are, without a mask, without pretending what you are not, because people feel it, people feel it when they want to pretend.

If you are haughty, pretending something you are not, or if you are humble, people will perceive it. By being grateful and humble you achieve many more things. That's the only thing I can advise you, transmit what you are in your networks, and I can guarantee you that the success will be incredible and I have the proof.

The networks have been for me the key to be in contact with my clients, to post the offers. They know they are going to eat, because I use my networks for that and without spending a lot of money. Get creative, there are many applications that help you to make it more beautiful, a frame, a name, use layers, there are great applications so you can post, create your logo, use your name, every time you post something try to put your company's logo, because that is what is running, that is what you are creating, your own name, your brand.

You must be very consistent. It's like in television, they tell you they want to do a contract, it must be a minimum of three or six months, because they know that it's the repetition that makes people recognize you.

So the same thing you are going to do, but in your social networks, repetitive, the same thing over and over again, so that they hear that name, your name, so many times, that they learn it. In our case, La Vecindad Pico de

Gallo, it is repetition and constancy what makes you reach the level of the greats.

An experience that happened to me recently also, with the owner of a very large business in Las Vegas, he approached me to ask me. He first praised my work in social media and asked me who I paid to do it. I told him that I don't pay anyone, that I do it. He was surprised and asked if I could teach him. Absolutely, I replied. I asked him to open his phone, we went on his page, and I told him what was right, what was wrong, what is free and what is not. Knowing that he has the money and the capabilities, I told him what I could do to make it free so he could reach more people faster. That cost me nothing and I was happy to do it.

So, I'm sharing it with you too. Use it, and it will help you to achieve many things.

Chapter 5

Forming a team

I learned to work a long time ago, but when you work with the client it is another thing, then it is what you also transmit to people, but suddenly you are not angry or anything, but people think you are angry. I once worked with a guy I met when I started, when I was working in the casino. They criticized me for having him working with me, because he came across as unfriendly. How can you have such a hateful person working here with you? I never answered them, rather, I would say: I'm going to talk to him, I'm working with him and I'm going to help him. And yes, I let him know what was going on, I let him know what the clients were saying.

He denied it, but I knew what was going on, I knew what his problem was, but I couldn't let him go because he had potential, which is what I want for my business. So, for a detail, for something so small that he can fix, I am not going to let him go.

He makes the decision, he fixes it and I know he can be the perfect employee, and he is now, because he made that decision, he realized how important perception is, what you convey to people and now he is working on that. In fact, my coach is the one who is working on this, helping me to make the process a little bit easier and he has already recognized it. By recognizing it and accepting it, it's already easier to guide him, it's already easier to talk, we're already on the same level.

When a person accepts what you are saying or those employees arrive who understand what you want, it is because you have already gone up a level of liberation and you begin to bring people to the same level that you are vibrating at that moment.

For example, a collaborator who started here from the beginning was growing with us. Luis, one of our employees, arrived, because we are also vibrating the same, he had a small defect, but that defect is something that I wanted to correct instead of getting rid of him, I preferred to help him to improve, because I know that he was going to be very beneficial for me, for my team, for my work, for my business. I have had to tell people to leave for being negative, for being problematic. When there is a negative work environment, things don't work.

I believe that all these people who are working with me right now have the necessary experience to know what they must do without me telling them.

The only thing I demand from them is quality and that they put their heart into it. What I need is that they make a team, instead of looking at whether the other one does or does not do it, correct him instead of coming to give me the finger, correct him if you see that the sauce is not good or he is doing it incorrectly, why do you keep quiet? Don't you see that this is going to affect you, not only me, but you, because if sales go down, I will not have enough money to pay, so who is better off getting the sauce right, you or me? That is what I tell you, so that is what you must take care of, that is what you have to watch out for, you yourselves to make sure that things go well, I say this to the team working in the back of the kitchen and I also say it to the people working in the front.

Your responsibility is that the people who are sitting here, who entered through that door, first, feel welcome, as soon as you open that door, after three seconds they enter, the first thing I want to hear is that they say welcome, good afternoon, the first thing they are not going to ask if it is to eat here or to take away, no! The first thing is to make them feel at home, say good morning, good afternoon, welcome, how may I help you. Make that person feel that where he/she has arrived, he/she is very well taken care of. That is where the quality of service can be seen.

So, it is not that they sit wherever they want, you are not going to receive them, you are going to welcome them, you are going to ask them what they like, if they have come before, you are going to suggest, I want them to ask why they came to us, how they heard about us, what they thought of our food.

Good or bad, at that moment, don't let him go away and after he walks through the door say what he liked, or he missed salt, or he makes a negative comment to someone else, why would he do it later, when you could have asked him inside, what he missed? Allow me a moment, I will fix it right away, you send him to make his dishes again, that's what I want, that's what you must pay attention to.

They are not going to bring out a dish if it does not have the presentation, if they must bring out a dish and they see it is wrong, why do they bring it out? If the cook must do it three times that is his fault, because he is not making sure that the food came out well.

So, we are a team from the door to the kitchen. It is the responsibility of the waiter if the dish arrives at the table, if it arrived well, if it didn't ask for onion, then why did you take it out with onion? You must pay attention to those little details because the customer will feel cared for. You greet your recurring customer and bring him a drink without him asking for a drink, if he comes every day to eat, why ask him? Immediately when you see him, you sit him down and bring him his drink to the table, that is a detail, that makes people say: "wow, they treat me better than at home".

So, remember that people, when they come to eat with us, are looking to have an experience, that we make them feel at home. That's my priority, both inside and out front.

We all have to worry about the little things that we think they're going to overlook. To me they are important, to many people they are not, but to me they are. It's not being picky, it's making sure that what I'm selling is the best; that's going to guarantee that I always have customers, that that customer comes back and that they bring more customers, because I'm giving the best.

You know what's nice? That my team understands that my team cares, the kitchen is impeccable, I don't have to worry about anything, because they are working with their hearts. Some call me boss, others call me patron or Vane. Vane, I cleaned up. This had fallen here, I found this, but I fixed it. They are my eyes, they are me in every different position in what they do, in everything they do, they are the ones who are going to be responsible for everything going well at the end of the day, because if we do well in the business, we all do well.

The reward is that they have never missed a paycheck, they have never missed a paycheck. Sometimes Raul and I had not yet received our first payment because we were working for the not-too-distant future, where we expected to receive our reward.

It is not easy. They get paid, whether there are sales or not, but for them to get paid, things must go well.

And sometimes it is difficult to have to tell an employee that unfortunately he has to leave, but there comes a moment when you become so strong that your passion for your business, the love you feel for what has cost you so much that makes you strong, is your patrimony, is what you are taking care of and you have the strength to tell him: unfortunately I cannot have you here anymore, it is hard, but there is a moment when you do it with satisfaction, because you take off a weight, like you take off something negative that was not right in your team.

They are little details that you think they are not, but they do cost a lot, it is the way to build what has cost you so much, so that is a very important part.

La Vecindad "Pico de Gallo" is my greatest satisfaction. Quality, service, and delivery with love is what it has meant to me to have the right team, at the right time and nothing more than knowing them, helping them and being grateful to them, because that is what you get in return, gratitude. That they value everything you are doing for them.

Chapter 6

Believing to create

In this time that we have been living this dream called La Vecindad "Pico de Gallo", I have witnessed many stories, many dreams, joys, and sorrows.

Everything we have seen come true is because we first believed in it. We did it with our hearts and it materialized in front of our eyes.

Believe to create, believe to do good things, believe to rise, to undertake, to help, to share without envy, be happy for your neighbor, be happy as I was always happy, and I thank everyone for the support.

I have had some experiences with clients that, in some ways have marked my life, and have given a special purpose to what we do in the business.

We just opened and I met one person. I was the only waitress, I had to bring up the dishes and well, doing what I like and talking to them, and I have become friends, we have become friends, and more than that, we became family.

I remember I met a couple, and the lady always came with a scarf on her head, she had cancer. It is hard to know that someone is sick with cancer and to understand what they are going through. But we were doing our part, in our services, accommodating her in what she could eat and what she could not eat, because she took very good care of herself.

There was contact between us, I never confessed to her that fear I felt of not knowing if maybe the time would come when I would not see her again, because they are regular customers. Practically since we opened, they have been our customers. When I had to bring my mother from Venezuela because she had cancer, they tried to help, they tried to share with me how to take care of my mother.

They even went to my house and, people who started out as a client and it becomes more than that. You have no one to turn to and they become that support, me for them and them for me. I thank them so much! I was always afraid I would never see them again. I will always thank them for reaching out to me and my family and I felt their support. They were my customers, but they became more than that.

In this process of our business, we have all had the opportunity to bring out the best in each other. Luis has also had the opportunity to grow; he began to study social communication, but has not been able to finish it and the fact that I have included him in my videos, that he is my partner when we do this type of advertising, just to see how he enjoys it, what he transmits, that for me is also very gratifying, to know that he is enjoying what he is doing and that also helps me to grow, because all that energy helps me to grow.

I know that we are going to do something else, although I still do not know how we are going to do it, I know that ideas and opportunities will come, and now we are preparing for it, because we started with only fourteen tables and now, we have twenty-five tables.

We are talking about production, more employees, more time, more dedication and I am not afraid of that, after everything I went through.

Now I feel the desire for it to be here, I am anxious to know what is coming, to keep growing, to keep preparing myself as a person.

I know that, as well as making me tough, it has made me smarter to handle situations, both financially and legally, and this is a constant preparation.

Every step you take is a step up, you are no longer down, we have already left behind what happened, we will continue to prepare ourselves because what is coming is big. Maybe there will not only be Vecindades around Las Vegas, but there will be Vecindades at a national level or, as one person put me on Tik Tok, in a video I uploaded when he said: imagine you setting up a Mexican restaurant in Venezuela!

Imagine me setting up a Vecindades also outside the United States, and that this becomes an empire, because we have created a different concept, we would already sell a brand, a franchise or that an investor comes, that a multimillionaire investor comes through that door and says he wants to invest in my business. Welcome!

The opportunities are open, and I know they will start to come, and we will see what is right for us, because they brought us this far and it doesn't end here. Sometimes, when people used to say to me to motivate me: "Can you imagine an investor arriving? Before I saw it far away, I saw it as a dream, who is going to look at me and my business? But now, where I am, after having achieved all that Raul and I have achieved, we can attest that at any moment an investor can come through that door, someone with money can come in.

I started with no money, if someone wants to invest in me, let them pay me for everything we have done, it sounds interesting. It blows my mind to know that we are going to have several locations locally, that's like I said, I used to see it as a dream, now I see it as opportunities that at any moment I know will present themselves.

We've already talked about it, it's already in our mind, it's already in our vocabulary of how we would handle small locations outside of our main headquarters.

I honestly don't know how it would be, but if I have achieved all this and we have overcome so many adversities, then, To the front, because to the back, not even to take impulse. There is no limit, and I am doing what I like, and I know that there is more to come, not only for me, but for my family, for my children, there is a heritage that I will inherit from them and that we will be recognized as something different.

The fact that I am writing my testimony of everything we have been through and that now I can properly say that I am happy for what I have achieved and for what is to come, is a success. To be called for interviews, to be wanted to interview me among so many businesses, there being so many casinos, is really flattering.

When they called me for the first time to tell me that I had won the nomination for "Best of Las Vegas", they told me: I can't tell you who won, I can only say that you won a gold and four bronze, the only thing I can tell you and to make you feel proud and well and to make you feel good, is that a small business never gets so many nominations, a small business never gets more than two and you got five, that's all I'm going to tell you.

When this gentleman told me that, I thought it is incredible to be recognized at a local level! And it is a recognition that is going to take me where I have not reached with my networks, to people who read the newspaper, who read the press, to other types of customers, and that other type of customers when they come and

91

see that this is a totally different experience, will take me to other people and I know that this will force me to be in more places to continue growing for what I am offering as a company, for what I am offering to them as a restaurant, and that is another challenge.

It's not just a matter of coming, opening a business and we've arrived; they are challenges, so we must keep growing, we have to keep overcoming them, we have to keep breaking obstacles. I am super proud, super happy, I never imagined how my story was going to be, that it was going to inspire others and that national television would look for me for that, that my Coach Patricia Hernández Carrillo would tell me: I want you to tell your story, it must be for something.

So, let's keep preparing ourselves. Just as we opened that champagne for that first award, we will open many more for those that came and those that will come, because the desire is there, this is just the beginning, this is just the beginning. And we continue to generate more prizes.

Everything I told you is the beginning of success, where I am now, we are preparing ourselves, we are studying, we are growing, we are doing everything possible to move forward for this to be a complete success, I sincerely thank my husband, my children, my coach for having believed in me, for having given me the opportunity.

I don't know why, but it came at the right time. I recommend you just let yourself be helped, everything is coming, the solutions come by themselves, you do not have to drown in a glass of water, if success is for you, even if you take off or put on, it will reach you, and even more if you are fighting for your dreams.

You go ahead because you are going to make it, it is to be great, to be important, to be a businesswoman, to be badass if you can, and I am the proof of it. From being an employee for many years, to having my own business is a success. I invite you to do it, grow, I am ready for what is coming, for the next step, the investor.

They tell me out there to write books, to do motivational talks, but there is a lot to tell, there is a lot to transmit, there is a lot to inspire and if we share and keep moving this energy, which is a circle, and it is like an avalanche. Imagine if we all unite with all this positive energy, who is going to beat us? So let's focus on what is good, let's focus on getting ahead, let's focus on growing and the change is in you, the change is in you, in that you want to be different, as I said at the beginning: be different, be you, grow and everything comes to you on a silver platter, because you deserve it, because what I am receiving now I deserve it for all that I have been through, for all that I worked, for all that sacrifice that Raul and I made from the beginning, two or three jobs.

Success is there. Let us go after it. Although I have not yet reached the top, I feel that there is more and I am not satisfied with what I have now, there is still more and I hope that soon I can tell you that I achieved that something more that will finish filling me and tell you what I was and for this I got here, it is what I am waiting for, it is what I am ready to receive and I am very happy to receive it.

My heart, mind and hands are open to move forward, we keep fighting, we keep growing, I don't really know how, but I know that La Vecindad keeps growing, keeps creating a magical little place out there and you will hear more from us, you will hear more, you will keep hearing about it, something else is going to happen. I will tell you later what happened, because I believe in that, I believe in what I am attracting to my business, what the energy of my business is attracting here.

I ask that success keeps us humble, keeps us down to earth and always with a good heart, and that's all there is to it. That's the most important idea, the most important secret that I think I've always tried to keep and have always kept: humility is being yourself and believing in yourself, so that we can keep going forward. That has been the key to my growth, and to keep fighting to inspire and motivate, to make my children proud of everything we did and what we are doing.

I know that the day is not far away when I will have the opportunity to share what happened, because we are close, and it won't be long now.

It is not that I don't have any stoppers, or maybe I break them myself now, but I know that we have to look for that something else that is missing, there is a purpose, and we have to look for that purpose. We are here and the right people are arriving, and we will continue to work hard, creating an empire.

I managed to remove all those obstacles that were in my way, what is coming is not scary, so here I am strong and ready to do whatever it takes to make my business a successful business. This is what I have wanted to happen, what I have been trying to visualize all this time.

I want to thank you all for the support you have given us and for all the love you have brought us this far. I know that someday my children will read this, and I want them to feel proud of everything they have gone through with their parents, to say: my parents were great, and that we did it, to say: we have a very cool thing, it is "La Vecindad Pico de Gallo".

It is a dream come true, the American dream, to be in another country, what you could not do in your country, to do it in one that is not yours, that is the first challenge.

As they say, you are not a prophet in your own land, Raul and I are the irrefutable proof that it is true, whether here or anywhere in the world, it can be done. And if we must start again, we do it, but with the experience and the faith that we are going to do it great.

Chapter 7

The cherry on the cake

In 2021 we positioned the brand, we positioned the neighborhood, this makes me feel proud, we opened a new section. The reception of the people has been beautiful, we have done in numbers what we had never done before, we have a wonderful team, the right people have come to work with us. As I see it, people who vibrate at the same frequency as we do, people who work out of passion, out of affection, who do it for love, not for the sake of collecting a check, and I think that has been the secret of La Vecindad's success.

After these awards a year ago, the year flew by, but it has been beautiful. First, because of the goals we set for ourselves and to see in numbers that we met and surpassed them.

People began to arrive automatically to La Vecindad, because they already knew what it was, they wanted to be here, to live the experience of being here, and that is what we achieved. We started to have the boys dress up as the characters of La Vecindad every Sunday, it was expanding, a beautiful energy was being created and the pieces were coming together.

One of the wonderful things that happened was that Facebook contacted me to tell me if I wanted to be part of an event that they were going to have because La Vecindad was a member of the Facebook Leaders Network, where I was going to tell my experience to the Senator of my State.

The only thing I thought about was my English, I never thought about the magnitude of what it meant. They confirmed by mail and told me that I was going to have a Zoom Meeting with Nevada Senator Catherine Cortez Masto.

I met with her and five other six small businesses here in Las Vegas that are also members of the Facebook Leaders Network and my biggest surprise when we got to the Zoom Meeting, the guy connected me and said: Ok Vanessa, you are the only lady, so you are going to start.

Do me start? I felt like a chick, we are talking about established American business owners, recognized here in Las Vegas and I had no contact with them, what am I going to say?

The only thing I know how to do is to tell my story and at that moment we are introduced, the Senator arrives, she was voting on a bill that is going to pass and she took 15-20 minutes to go to this meeting.

She comes in, introduces me, says: Hello Vanessa, how are you? I tell her about the neighborhood and that we started in the Swapmeet, that we have been growing, and that thanks to the economic support that the government gave to small businesses we were able to survive because my fear when we closed in the pandemic was how we were going to pay the rent and all those things and I told her about my whole process, that I was able to pay my rent and that at that time, when I applied for those emergency loans we were very few employees because I received a minimal amount but that minimal amount for me was a lot.

I thanked him for that minimal support because that support helped me to be here, he asked me where in Las Vegas was my business and I told him that it was in the Historic Mall.

He told me: When I was a child I used to go to that mall. So you have lifted that up, you make me proud that you have lifted up that area of town. It was very neglected in that area here in Las Vegas. -I said: Yes, when we arrived it was a very difficult one. There was prostitution and as people began to arrive, they were being driven away, because there was already a commercial movement.

He said: Vanessa, I loved talking to you, I loved your story. I promise that when I go to Las Vegas I will visit you. -I said: "Ok! But I did not take it seriously. She is at the congress, what is she going to look at my business?

After me, about two or three people spoke; she had to go back, so, out of the whole group, I was the one who spoke the most, telling my story.

When the next person came in, he spoke more technical words, more uninhibited, more about numbers, and I thought: What a shame! And so it was, the meeting ended, and the senator's assistant thanked us.

My biggest surprise was that the following week, the assistant spoke to me: We have a question, the senator wants to visit your restaurant, but it will be something private. We do not want to invite the mass because it is something more political. If a lot of people come in, it will be discrediting; we just want small businesses that were helped by the government to get ahead in times of pandemic.

I told him: Of course!

He clarified: There will only be a certain number of people as journalists, there will be television and other media and social networks, but we do not want a lot of people. What would be the possibilities of doing it this way? - I told her: what I can do is to close a room and we can offer them breakfast and she can talk to the other small businesses, and it is already something intimate, and we can control the entrance.

The day came and while she was inside, I never let any customers in. The senator was fascinated with the place, in fact, she signed the wall; there is her signature that augurs us success and prosperity.

A few days ago, another assistant from Washington called me again thanking me because I also did an interview for the local Hispanic newspaper El Tiempo, where they asked me how the pandemic experience had been. I told the truth, the same thing I told the

Senator, I told them, and the Senator sent me to thank me for having given that interview, for the favor that had been done with small businesses.

She is a very noble lady, she told me that there is a possibility that they would call me back for another interview, if I was willing. I told her that whenever she liked I was at her disposal.

That is one of the spectacular things that happened, the senator was here in my restaurant.

Sometime ago I received an email from a company saying that since we were using their name: Pico de Gallo, they would be monitoring us for the use of their brand.

To be honest, I was concerned. Since, I was doing the name for someone else, here in Vegas. That at any moment they would come to tell me that they would open a restaurant in Las Vegas or that I would have to pay them for the use of their name. So, that is when I made the decision to register our own name. Which meant changing everything and more importantly our customers would be confused by the change. Which didn't stop me and I registered the trademark LA VECINDAD® and our phrase PICA, PERO PERO NO MUERDE®. After a long time of waiting, we managed to patent our name and phrase, we are now a REGISTERED TRADEMARK!

Then I received a call, it was something in English. At the time I did not understand what they were saying, but they wanted to record my restaurant and I authorized them to do so.

I was open to whatever came, to whatever was presented, but at that moment I did not see the magnitude of what it meant. Later, when I paid attention, when they started asking questions, I realized that it was Food Paradise, a television production company that does episodes of food and spectacular places. They wanted to record an episode here in the restaurant and this episode was going to be on Food Network, Discovery Channel, Travel Channel and there were going to be two versions, a national version and an international version.

Obviously, I said yes, the only thing they asked me was to close for one day. That means to stop producing, to stop receiving money, but I did not mind. It was worth the price, I had to risk something. They said to me: "Is a weekend okay with you? I told them that weekends are particularly good for me, and I can't close on a Saturday or Sunday, because it means a lot in terms of numbers, but if you give me a day during the week, I'd be very happy to do it. And they accepted!

Two weeks later it all came together. They came to record the episode; it was filled with television equipment; my restaurant was a recording set. We felt that the camera operators, the director, the producer, they were all very nice people, and they were impressed with what we were doing.

We introduced them to what we do, the Cuban cakes, the café de olla, we told our story.

Our Café de Olla has been especially important in our positioning. Raul started making this coffee every day, in the traditional way as his grandmother taught him. On one occasion a friend, Chef Piero, visited us and was delighted with our coffee. He was fascinated by the idea of serving it in clay cups and suggested that we put a little cinnamon and sugar on the rim of the cup. We then added a little piece of cinnamon to complement the presentation, and since then, our coffee has been an icon of the Vecindad!

He said, "I want to interview you. There is going to be a moment when we are going to sit you down and you're going to talk. (Oh, my God!) They sat me down and asked me questions. Raul did not want to come out because he is shy. I want them to recognize him because he is my friend, he is my partner and he told me: yes, we are going to do it. And we went out like he and I were the creators of this. The most beautiful thing was that when I was in the interview, the producer said to me: Vanessa, how do you know what experience people have when they come to eat here? And I told him: For me you see it, you feel it, in fact, I have the answer right there at the door. The producer turned around and said to me: "What does it say there? I read him the text: If you liked the service and the food, ring the bell. -He said: Wonderful!

They told me that after Christmas 2021 they were going to release the episode. They spent the whole day recording from 7 in the morning until 6 in the evening and the last thing they recorded was they had the crew sitting down, eating as if they were customers, and he rings the bell and we, what we say to people when they ring the bell is, "thank you" or "thank you," and it ended the recording. I am sure that part of the episode is going to come out.

The main dish: the Cuban cake and there is going to be an international version. We were asked to make the café de olla and a sauce that Luis made in a hot Molcajete, which turned out spectacular!

He made it there, with the stone, and that version is the one that will go to the international level, in other words, we are going to be at the world level. This is where I say: we positioned ourselves this year, it was the recognition that we exist, that we are there, that we make noise, that people from other restaurants have commented to us that we are already competition for them and we have never thought that we are competition for anyone, but they see us as competition. We are talking about renowned restaurants here in Las Vegas, because people have a birthday and they go to that restaurant, because they are going to celebrate. We do not have alcohol yet and we have achieved all this without alcohol.

All this magic and all this result we have done with the magic that is lived here, the vibe that you feel from the moment you enter, when you eat and when you leave.

To close with a flourish, we were informed that, out of the 23 categories that we had been nominated in the summer for: "The Best of Las Vegas", we won 13 nominations! Among them 7 golds, for us the most important was the best Mexican food in Las Vegas.

The first time we won was last year, but we won that category in bronze, first place went to a well-known restaurant, second place to a casino and we were in third place, competing with large industries, with casinos.

When the person from the newspaper called me, he told me: I repeat the same as last year, I do not know what you do, but it is impressive how you are doing it, because winning 7 golds, silvers and bronze in a total of 13, is something exceptional!

We always like to create, even in decoration. We all get to paint, add even if it is a plant, or whatever it takes to make it look good.

Now we are overhauling the kitchen to make it flow more quickly. Our kitchen is small for what we serve, and people imagine it's huge, but it's not. We are working to make our customers feel better served and little by little we are achieving this.

You must believe in order to create and not doubt. Be focused on visualizing that what is coming, because you don't know how it will materialize in some way, and that, from all the work you do, sooner or later, you will reap its fruits.

You should not give up. When we wanted to throw in the towel, Coach Patricia Hernández Carrillo arrived and helped us. Sometimes everything comes together, the business is just starting, and it does not work out, family problems start, finding employees, everything becomes difficult, you think you are not going to make it and what happens is that you run away. I think that is why many businesses don't get off the ground, they don't make it past the second year.

Right now, our team is made up of 20 employees and we already have our first manager, by merit and dedication, Luis Islas!

It has been very gratifying because we paid the price, we had to train ourselves, try, have discipline. People who are starting out come and the most beautiful thing is that they tell you: "you inspire me", and that this serves as an inspiration for all those people who want to undertake, who want to get ahead because we come from below, we are not from a cradle, we had no money, we had nothing, and to demonstrate that, despite the adversities, yes you can do it!

Made in the USA
Monee, IL
21 February 2022